I0425839

December 2012

LOW-INCOME HOUSING TAX CREDITS

Agencies Implemented Changes Enacted in 2008, but Project Data Collection Could Be Improved

GAO
Accountability ★ Integrity ★ Reliability

December 2012

LOW-INCOME HOUSING TAX CREDITS

Agencies Implemented Changes Enacted in 2008, but Project Data Collection Could Be Improved

Why GAO Did This Study

IRS and state HFAs administer the LIHTC program, the largest source of federal assistance for developing affordable rental housing. HFAs are allocated tax credits on a per capita basis and award them to developers. By acquiring project equity from developers, investors may become eligible for the credits, which offset federal tax liabilities. As part of HERA, Congress made changes to the program that included increasing credits allocated to states, setting a temporary floor on the most common LIHTC rate (the portion of eligible project costs for which a developer can receive credits), and giving HFAs more discretion in "enhancing" (i.e., increasing) awards. HERA also required GAO to study the changes, including the distribution of credit allocations before and after HERA. This report discusses (1) how IRS and selected HFAs implemented the HERA changes, (2) what HUD's data show about the number and characteristics of projects completed from 2006 through 2010 and any data limitations, and (3) stakeholders' views on the effects of the HERA changes on LIHTC projects. GAO reviewed IRS and state guidelines, analyzed HUD data on LIHTC projects, and spoke with federal, state, and industry officials.

What GAO Recommends

GAO recommends that HUD evaluate and implement additional steps to improve its LIHTC Database. HUD agreed with the recommendation but said the report could better describe the agency's efforts to improve data collection despite resource constraints. In response, GAO added further information on HUD's changes to its collection process.

View GAO-13-66. For more information, contact Daniel Garcia-Diaz at (202) 512-8678 or garciadiazd@gao.gov or James R. White at (202) 512-9110 or whitej@gao.gov.

What GAO Found

Federal and state agencies implemented changes made in 2008 to the Low-Income Housing Tax Credit (LIHTC) program by revising program guidance and modifying plans for allocating tax credits. The Internal Revenue Service (IRS) implemented the changes made by the Housing and Economic Recovery Act of 2008 (HERA) by, among other things, issuing notices and revenue procedures. Program stakeholders that GAO contacted said that IRS's actions were generally sufficient. But as of October 2012, IRS and the Department of the Treasury were still working on implementation issues, such as developing guidance on the provision designed to ease restrictions on using tax credits to acquire existing federally or state-assisted buildings. At the state level, housing finance agencies (HFA) implemented the HERA changes by modifying their tax credit allocation plans, which provide criteria for awarding credits. For example, in their plans, some HFAs cited financial need as the only criterion for awarding HERA-created enhanced credits. Others planned to target specific types of projects, such as those using "green building" practices.

The Department of Housing and Urban Development (HUD) voluntarily compiles the largest public database on LIHTC projects, but the data it collects from HFAs are incomplete. Despite HUD efforts to improve its data collection process, the database may undercount projects, in part because HUD did not follow up on potentially incomplete information. For example, HUD's database showed that one state had between 23 and 49 completed projects each year from 2006 through 2009, but only 2 projects in 2010. However, officials from this state's HFA provided GAO with documentation showing that they had reported 37 projects for 2010. Further, much of the project data that HUD has received does not include characteristics such as the type of location, construction, and tenants targeted. A HUD official noted that a HERA provision requiring states to collect tenant-level data (e.g., race and income) had made collecting project data more challenging because HUD did not receive additional resources and available resources had to be divided between tenant and project data collection. Without more complete data on the LIHTC program, the federal government's ability to evaluate basic program outcomes—such as how much housing was produced—and overall federal efforts to provide affordable housing may suffer. Data from 42 HFAs that reported each year from 2006 through 2010 provide limited insight into the actual number and characteristics of LIHTC projects. The number of reported projects completed exceeded 5,300, and most were in metropolitan areas and were new construction. However, missing data prevented analysis of trends over the 5-year period. For example, the proportion of missing information on the types of tenants targeted increased from 5 percent in 2006 to 28 percent in 2010.

Program stakeholders told GAO that the broad effects of the HERA provisions on the LIHTC market were difficult to determine but noted that certain provisions enhanced the financial feasibility of some individual projects. For example, stakeholders said the temporary increase in per capita credit allocations, temporary credit rate floor, and discretion to use enhanced credits improved the financial viability of some projects by allowing states to award more credits per project. Some state officials also said that the larger awards especially benefited projects in rural areas that can be difficult to finance because they tend to have lower rents and are less attractive to investors than projects in urban areas.

_____ **United States Government Accountability Office**

Contents

Figures

United States Government Accountability Office
Washington, DC 20548

December 6, 2012

The Honorable Max Baucus
Chairman
The Honorable Orrin G. Hatch
Ranking Member
Committee on Finance
United States Senate

The Honorable Dave Camp
Chairman
The Honorable Sander Levin
Ranking Member
Committee on Ways and Means
House of Representatives

The Low-Income Housing Tax Credit (LIHTC) program is the largest federal program for building and rehabilitating rental housing that is affordable to low-income households. It is estimated to cost $6.5 billion in fiscal year 2012 in forgone revenue. The program is jointly administered by the Internal Revenue Service (IRS) and state housing finance agencies (HFA).[1] Each state receives an annual allocation of LIHTCs by statutory formula according to population.[2] HFAs then competitively award the tax credits to owners of qualified rental housing projects that reserve all or a portion of their units for low-income tenants. Developers typically attempt to obtain funding for their projects by attracting third-party investors that are willing to contribute equity to the projects, and the project investors can then claim the LIHTCs. This process of providing LIHTCs in exchange for equity is generally referred to as "selling" the tax credits.[3] The developers or investors can claim their share of credit each year during the 10-year credit period, which can be used to reduce their

---

[1]All 50 states, the District of Columbia, Puerto Rico, and four U.S. possessions (American Samoa, Guam, the Northern Mariana Islands, and the U.S. Virgin Islands) have HFAs that receive LIHTC allocations. HFAs are state-chartered authorities established to meet the affordable housing needs of the residents of their states.

[2]26 U.S.C. § 42(h)(3).

[3]The owners of the LIHTC project are permitted to claim the LIHTCs on their income tax return. Technically, what is sold to the investor is not the credit but an ownership interest in the project (through a partnership or other entity).

tax liability. Individual HFAs maintain data on the number of projects that receive tax credit allocations each year, as well as the characteristics of these projects. The Department of Housing and Urban Development (HUD) has almost no direct administrative responsibility for the LITHC program, but it voluntarily collects information from the HFAs on LIHTC projects for its LIHTC Database, which is the most comprehensive public source of information on LIHTC projects.

Since its inception in 1986, the program has helped to build or rehabilitate more than 36,000 projects that help provide housing for low-income households.[4] In 2008 and 2009—in the midst of the financial crisis—the program was severely disrupted when investor demand for tax credits collapsed and developers could not obtain funding for projects that would have qualified for the credit. The onset of financial struggles for large banks and the exit of two large LIHTC investors from the LIHTC market—Fannie Mae and Freddie Mac—contributed greatly to decreased investor demand.[5] During that period, Congress took a number of actions to improve the operation of the LIHTC program, including changes enacted as part of the Housing and Economic Recovery Act of 2008 (HERA).[6] These changes generally went into effect after July 30, 2008, including

---

[4]Although the LIHTC program is a major source of financing for affordable rental housing, some researchers have argued that the program may displace other affordable housing that would have been available through the private, unsubsidized housing market. A 2008 report by the Congressional Research Service reviewed the research literature on this and other issues concerning the impact of the LIHTC program. Congressional Research Service, *The Low-Income Housing Tax Credit: A Framework for Evaluation*, RL33904 (Washington, D.C.: Apr. 15, 2008).

[5]Fannie Mae and Freddie Mac are private, federally chartered companies created by Congress to, among other things, provide liquidity to home mortgage markets by purchasing mortgage loans, thus enabling lenders to make additional loans. In September 2008, Fannie Mae and Freddie Mac were placed into federal government conservatorship.

[6]Pub. L. No. 110-289, 122 Stat. 2654 (July 30, 2008). Under the American Recovery and Reinvestment Act of 2009 (Pub. L. No. 111-5), Congress also created two new programs that addressed the lack of private investment in projects that would otherwise have used LIHTCs. The two programs are the Tax Credit Assistance Program and the Grants to States for Low-Income Housing Projects in Lieu of Low-Income Housing Credits Program. HFAs were to use the funding from these programs to provide gap financing for stalled "shovel-ready" projects and to offset the drop in the demand for, and subsequently the price of, LIHTCs. For information on the implementation of these programs, see GAO, *Recovery Act: Opportunities to Improve Management and Strengthen Accountability over States' and Localities' Uses of Funds*, GAO-10-999 (Washington, D.C.: Sept. 20, 2010) and *Recovery Act: Housing Programs Met Spending Milestones, but Asset Management Information Needs Evaluation*, GAO-12-634 (Washington, D.C.: June 18, 2012).

specific changes for projects placed in service—that is, suitable for occupancy—after July 30, 2008.[7]

HERA also required us to study and report on the implementation of the changes, including analyzing the distribution of credit allocations before and after the changes went into effect.[8] This report discusses (1) how IRS and selected HFAs implemented the HERA changes to the LIHTC program, (2) what HUD's data on LIHTC projects show about the number and characteristics of projects completed from 2006 through 2010 and any data limitations, and (3) the views of program stakeholders about the effects of the HERA changes on these projects.

To assess how IRS and HFAs implemented the HERA provisions, we reviewed IRS guidance, memorandums, and planning documents, as well as state qualified allocation plans (QAP), which contain detailed selection criteria and application requirements for the LIHTC program. We also interviewed officials from IRS, the Department of the Treasury (Treasury), and nine HFAs about the implementation of these changes.[9] We selected the 9 HFAs (out of the 56 that receive LIHTC allocations) to cover different geographic regions and allocation amounts, but their experiences are not representative of all states. To describe HUD's LIHTC data and what these data show about the number and characteristics of LIHTC projects, we analyzed information contained in HUD's LIHTC Database, which was last updated in July 2012.[10] We conducted reasonableness checks on the data to identify any missing, erroneous, or outlying figures. We also interviewed HUD about how it and its contractor compile the data. These steps revealed that the data were not complete, which limited what we could conclude from our data analysis. Using the HUD data that were available, we examined the types

---

[7]IRS Notice 88-116 defines the placed-in-service date as the date on which the first unit in the building is certified as being suitable for occupancy under state or local law.

[8]HERA at § 3004. The program changes within the scope of our review are contained in HERA, div. C, title I, subtitle A, 122 Stat. 2878-2888 (July 30, 2008).

[9]We interviewed HFA officials from California, Florida, Massachusetts, Michigan, Minnesota, North Carolina, Oregon, Texas, and Vermont.

[10]The LIHTC data that IRS maintains are oriented toward enforcing the tax code rather than measuring program outcomes. Although not an administering agency, HUD has historically collected information on projects produced under the program due to the importance of LIHTCs as a source of funding for low-income housing. The most recent data available from the database are for properties placed in service in 2010.

and locations of projects that states supported with their tax credit allocations, including the proportions of projects that were in rural versus urban areas, that were newly constructed versus acquired, and that were targeted to specific kinds of tenants. In addition, we used the National Council of State Housing Agencies' (NCSHA) annual HFA Factbooks from 2006 through 2010 to analyze the extent to which developers returned credits that had not been exchanged for equity to the states. We assessed the reliability of the HUD and NCSHA data and concluded that these data were sufficiently reliable for our reporting objective. To obtain the views of selected HFAs and industry participants about the effect of the HERA changes on LIHTC projects, we interviewed the same nine HFAs, as well as industry associations, investors, syndicators, and housing developers. We also reviewed supporting documentation from these entities about their views. Appendix I contains additional details about our scope and methodology.

We conducted this performance audit from February through December 2012 in accordance with generally accepted government auditing standards. Those standards require that we plan and perform the audit to obtain sufficient, appropriate evidence to provide a reasonable basis for our findings and conclusions based on our audit objectives. We believe that the evidence obtained provides a reasonable basis for our findings and conclusions based on our audit objectives.

Background

Description of the LIHTC Program

LIHTCs follow a multistep process that begins with the allocation of tax credits to HFAs. The process of allocating, awarding, and using LIHTCs is depicted in figure 1.

Figure 1: Key Steps and Entities in the LIHTC Process

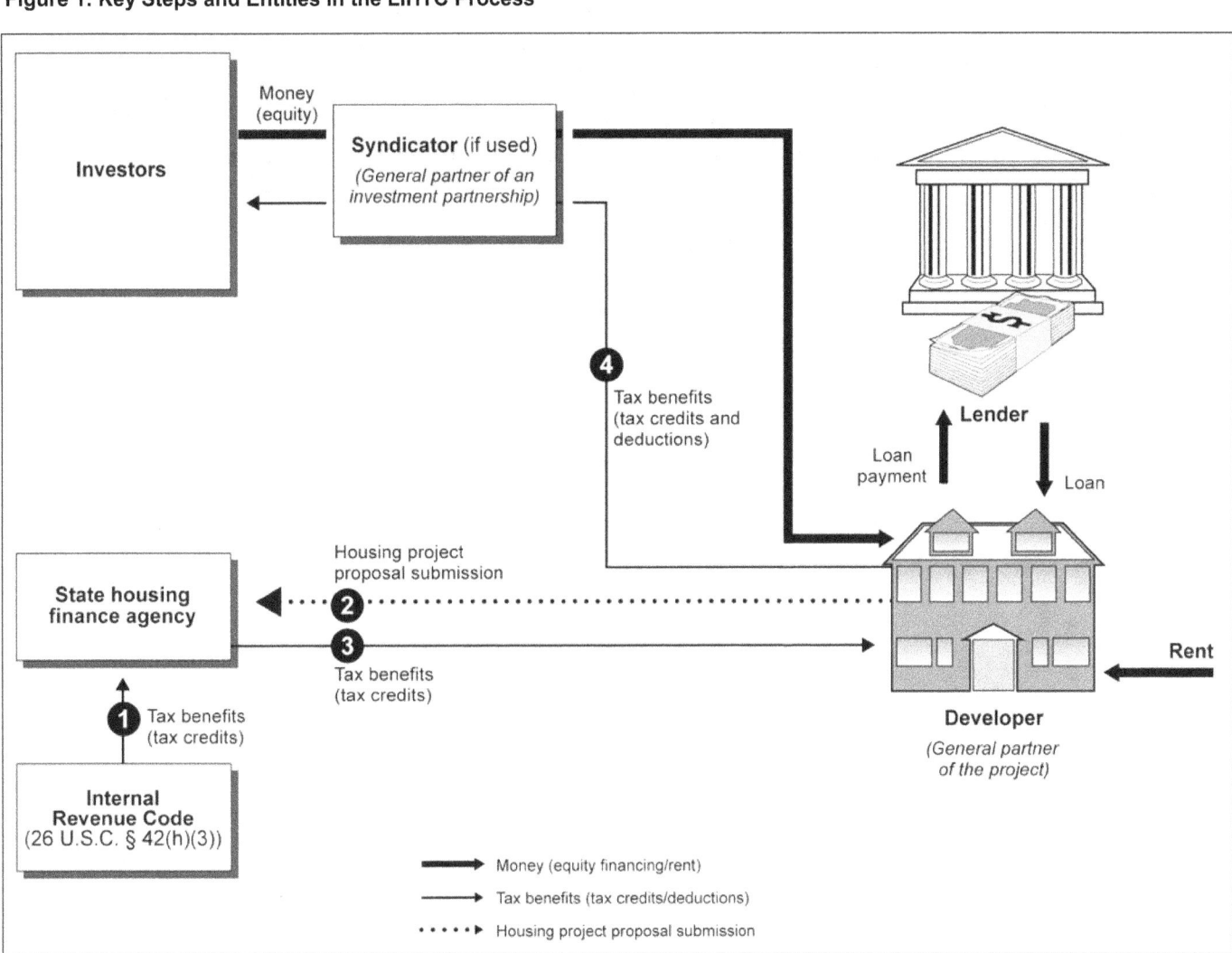

Source: GAO.

Note: For a more complete description and an additional graphic on the LIHTC oversight and compliance system, see GAO, *Opportunities to Improve Oversight of the Low-Income Housing Program*, GAO/GGD/RCED-97-55 (Washington, D.C.: Mar. 27, 1997).

As the figure shows, there are four primary steps in the LIHTC process.

1. *HFAs receive tax credit allocations.* State ceilings for LIHTCs are allocated by statutory formula to states annually according to

population, with a minimum amount awarded to states with small populations.[11] For 2012, the formula was $2.20 per capita or a minimum of $2,525,000.[12]

2. *Developers apply to the states for tax credits.* To apply for tax credits, a developer must submit a detailed proposal to an HFA. To qualify for consideration, a project must meet certain requirements, such as reserving specified percentages of available units for lower income households and restricting rents for these households to 30 percent of a calculated income limit.

3. *HFAs award tax credits to selected housing projects.* The potential to earn tax credits is competitively awarded to housing projects in accordance with states' QAPs. QAPs outline a state's affordable housing priorities and set out its procedure for ranking the projects on the basis of how well they meet state priorities and selection criteria that are appropriate to local conditions. The QAP must give preference to projects that serve the tenants with the lowest incomes, serve qualifying tenants for the longest period of time, and are located in a qualified census tract (QCT) and contribute to a local community revitalization plan.[13] Developers receiving tax credit allocations have 2 years to complete their projects and may not claim the credits until the projects are placed in service.

4. *Investors receive tax benefits.* Investment partnerships are a primary source of equity financing for LIHTC projects. Syndicators recruit investors willing to become partners in LIHTC partnerships. The money investors pay for the partnership interest is paid into the LIHTC project as equity financing. Although investors are buying an interest in a rental housing partnership, this process is commonly referred to as buying tax credits because they receive tax credits in return for their investment. Once the LIHTC project is placed in service, or ready

---

[11]26 U.S.C. § 42(h)(3).

[12]The state ceiling applies to (1) the 9 percent credit for nonfederally subsidized new buildings and substantially rehabilitated buildings treated as new buildings, and (2) the 4 percent credit for acquired buildings. The state credit ceiling does not include the 4 percent credit available to housing projects financed with tax-exempt bonds, which are associated with private activity bonds.

[13]Under 26 U.S.C. § 42(d)(5)(B)(ii)(I), QCTs are designated by the Secretary of Housing and Urban Development and include census tracts where either 50 percent or more of households have income below 60 percent of the area median gross income or the poverty rate is at least 25 percent.

for occupancy, investors can receive their share of the credits each year of the 10-year credit period and can use the credit to offset federal income taxes otherwise owed on their tax returns, as long as the project meets the LIHTC requirements.

The amount of tax credits a project can receive depends on several factors, including the applicable fraction and the applicable percentage (see table 1). The applicable fraction, or the percentage of units in the building considered to be qualified low-income units, is the lesser of (1) the total square feet of the low-income units divided by the total square feet of all the units, or (2) the number of the low-income units divided by the total number of units. Regarding the applicable percentage, there are two credit rates (referred to as the 9 percent and 4 percent rates) for the LIHTC program that determine how much of a project's costs the allocated credits can cover. The credit rate takes into account whether the project is newly constructed or acquired and rehabilitated and the extent to which it uses other federal subsidies.[14] Most new construction and substantial rehabilitation projects are eligible for the 9 percent rate, which allows investors to claim credits for about 9 percent of the eligible basis annually over a 10-year period.[15] Prior to HERA, the actual percentage for the 9 percent credit floated based on a statutory formula and often fell below 9 percent.

---

[14]The 9 percent credit is also known as the 70 percent present value credit. 26 U.S.C. § 42(b). This latter terminology reflects the fact that the 9 percent credit is designed to yield a total amount over the 10-year credit period that is worth 70 percent of the present value of the stream of tax credits. The 9 percent rate refers to the approximate value that can be claimed by investors each year.

[15]Investors use the 4 percent credit for acquisition of existing buildings and new construction projects that are financed in conjunction with tax-exempt bonds and other gap subsidies. The 4 percent credit floats based on a statutory formula.

Table 1: Example of LIHTC Calculation

1. Total project development cost	$11,500,000
2. Ineligible costs (e.g., land acquisition, cash reserves, syndication costs, certain financing costs)	(1,500,000)
3. Eligible basis (row 1 - row 2) (Construction costs, architects' fees, environmental surveys, relocation expenses, title and recording fees, appraisals)	$10,000,000
4. Applicable fraction (In this example, all units in the project are low-income units)	100%
5. Qualified basis (row 3 x row 4)	$10,000,000
6. Applicable percentage	9%
7. Annual credit amount taken over 10 years (row 4 x row 5)	**$900,000**
8. Credits over 10 years	**$9,000,000**

Source: GAO analysis.

The amount of equity an investor is willing to contribute to the construction of the project in exchange for credits results in the effective price of an ownership interest in the project. In the above example, if the investor made $6,750,000 in total equity contributions, the implied price of the credits would be $0.75 for each dollar of credit ($6,750,000/$9,000,000).[16]

HERA Changes to the LIHTC Program

HERA made more than 20 changes to the LIHTC program that generally became effective after July 30, 2008.[17] Table 2 provides brief descriptions of the changes discussed in this report. Appendix II lists all of the changes to the LIHTC program made by the Multi-Family Housing subtitle of HERA.

---

[16]For additional information on the calculation of the price of LIHTC credits, see GAO, *Community Reinvestment Act: Challenges in Quantifying Its Effect on Low-Income Housing Tax Credit Investment*, GAO-12-869R (Washington, D.C.: Aug. 28, 2012).

[17]HERA, div. C, title I, subtitle A, 122 Stat. 2878-2888 (July 30, 2008).

Table 2: HERA Changes Discussed in This Report

HERA change	Description
1. Temporarily increased per capita credit allocations to states	Before HERA, the amount of credits a state received was based on a formula that adjusted the 2003 per capita rate of $1.75 for inflation. In 2003, states with small populations received at least $2,030,000 in allocations, also adjusted for inflation each subsequent year. HERA increased the per capita allocation by 10 percent for 2008—from $2.00 to $2.20—which resulted in a per capita allocation of $2.30 in 2009 after adjusting for inflation. The allocation for states with small populations was increased to $2,555,000 in 2008 ($2,665,000 in 2009, adjusted for inflation). After 2009, the per capita allocations reverted to the amounts that would have been specified by the inflation calculations ($2.10 and $2,430,000 in 2010).
2. Established a 9 percent minimum credit rate	Before HERA, the actual percentages for the 9 percent credit floated based on a statutory formula and often fell below 9 percent. HERA set a floor of 9 percent for this credit, effective for buildings placed in service after July 30, 2008 and before December 31, 2013. Without this provision, the rate would have been 7.94 percent for August 2008.
3. Gave states flexibility to pick buildings eligible for a "basis boost"	HERA gave HFAs the ability to designate any building, regardless of location, as eligible for an enhanced credit of up to 130 percent of the building's eligible basis (rather than the normal 100 percent), in effect treating these projects as if they were in a difficult development area or a qualified census tract.[a] HERA required HFAs to find that the basis boost was necessary for a building to be financially feasible as part of a qualified project before granting it to a developer.
4. Redefined when a building is considered federally subsidized	Before HERA, if any part of a building's eligible basis was federally subsidized, the building was ineligible for the 9 percent credit. HERA limited the definition of a federal subsidy for these purposes to tax-exempt bonds, thus possibly making more buildings eligible for the 9 percent credit.
5. Eased restrictions on using LIHTCs to acquire an existing building	Before HERA, in general, the acquisition costs for an existing building would not be eligible for the credit unless there was a period of at least 10 years between the date it was acquired by the taxpayer and the date the building was last placed in service. HERA waived the 10-year rule for any federally or state-assisted building. A federally assisted building is a building "substantially" assisted, financed, or operated under specific sections of various housing acts or under any other housing program administered by HUD or by the Department of Agriculture's Rural Housing Service. A state-assisted building is a building "substantially" assisted, financed, or operated under any state law with purposes similar to one of the acts just mentioned.
6. Repealed the bond posting requirement	Before HERA, a taxpayer could avoid credit recapture when disposing of a building by posting a disposition bond with IRS. The purpose of the bond was to ensure the recapture amount could be assessed and collected if a recapture event occurred after the disposition. HERA replaced this option by extending a statute of limitations for assessing the recapture amount to 3 years from the date the taxpayer notifies Treasury (IRS) that noncompliance with federal LIHTC requirements has occurred, if it is reasonably expected that such building will continue to be a qualified low-income building for the remainder of the compliance period.[b] Although generally applicable to dispositions of a building after HERA's enactment date, at the election of the taxpayer, the provision also applies to dispositions on or before that date if the taxpayer had placed a disposition bond with IRS in a timely fashion.

HERA change	Description
7. Changed median income rules in rural areas	Before HERA, tenant income limits were based on the relevant area's median gross income. HERA changed the measurement of area median gross income applied to certain properties in certain rural areas so that the income limits for these properties would be measured by the greater of the otherwise applicable area median gross income or the national nonmetropolitan median gross income.
8. Changed the general public use requirement	To be eligible for LIHTCs, residential units in qualified projects must be available for general public use. HERA clarified that a project would not fail this requirement just because it favored tenants who had special needs, were members of specified groups, or were involved in artistic or literary activities.
9. Instituted hold harmless provisions for reductions in area median gross income	Before HERA, HUD used a "hold harmless" policy to keep the area median gross income it used to determine eligibility for HUD's main rental assistance program from falling. HERA put the HUD practice into the Internal Revenue Code to bolster the financial viability of LIHTC projects by preventing rents from automatically falling when the area median gross income level on which rents are based declined. It did this by adding hold harmless provisions to address areas where the area median gross income had decreased. HERA prevented future decreases in tenant income limits and rents resulting from declines in area median gross income.

Sources: GAO analysis of HERA changes; Joint Committee on Taxation, *General Explanation of Tax Legislation Enacted in the 110th Congress*, JCS-1-09 (March 2009); Michael J. Novogradac and Glenn A. Graff, "Impact of the Housing and Economic Recovery Act of 2008 on Current and Future Low-Income Housing Tax Credit Properties," *Journal of Affordable Housing & Community Development Law*, vol.18, no.1 (fall 2008).

Note: See appendix II for a list of all changes to the LIHTC program made by the Multi-Family Housing subtitle of HERA.

[a]A difficult development area is defined as "any area designated by the Secretary of Housing and Urban Development as an area which has high construction, land, and utility costs relative to area median gross income." HUD updates the list of such areas annually. 26 U.S.C § 42(d)(5)(B)(iii)(I).

[b]A LIHTC project is subject to a 15-year compliance period during which a taxpayer is subject to IRS oversight and an extended use period of at least 30 years during which the project is subject to HFA oversight. The 15-year compliance period and the extended use period begin at the same time. Noncompliance with federal LIHTC requirements within the 15-year compliance period may result in IRS's denying claims for the credit in the current year or recapturing credits claimed in prior years.

Other Economic and Program Changes Affecting LIHTC

In addition to HERA, several other economic and program developments affected the LIHTC program in the 2008 to 2009 time frame (see fig. 2). For example, the general economic recession beginning at the end of 2007 reduced the profitability of banks and other financial institutions that were large LIHTC investors. As a result, these investors had no need for tax credits because they experienced losses or lower profits and thus had lower tax liabilities to offset. With the drop in demand for the credits, the effective prices of LIHTCs fell, creating funding gaps for developers who had assumed they would be able to sell their tax credits for a higher price.

According to one report, thousands of projects and tens of thousands of units that would have otherwise been bought or rehabilitated stalled.[18]

Figure 2: Timeline of Key Events Affecting LIHTC Market, 2007 through 2009

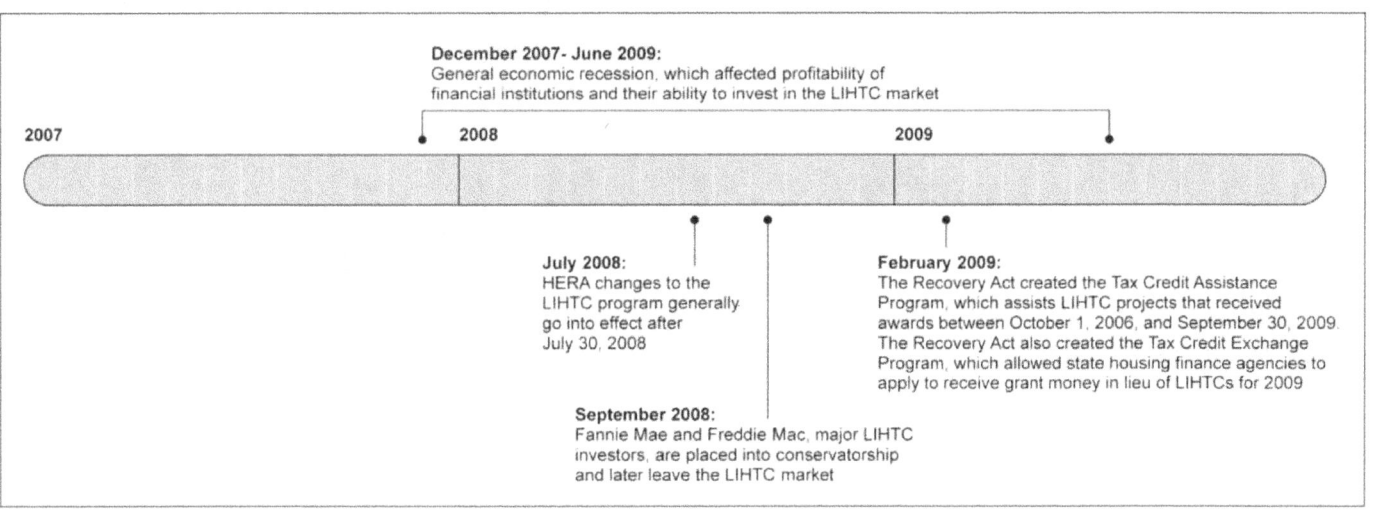

Source: GAO.

To help fill the funding gaps, in February 2009 Congress enacted the American Recovery and Reinvestment Act of 2009 (Recovery Act), which created the Tax Credit Assistance Program (TCAP) and the Tax Credit Exchange Program (Exchange Program). TCAP provided supplemental grant and loan funds to projects that received LIHTCs. The Exchange Program allowed HFAs the option of exchanging eligible portions of the state's housing credit ceiling for cash grants that could be used to finance low-income housing.

---

[18]Joint Center for Housing Studies of Harvard University, *The Disruption of the Low-Income Housing Tax Credit Program: Causes, Consequences, Responses, and Proposed Correctives* (Cambridge, Mass.: December 2009).

IRS Revised Guidance and States Modified Qualified Allocation Plans to Implement the HERA Changes

Because the LIHTC program is jointly administered by federal and state governments, agencies at both levels played roles in implementing HERA's changes to the program. At the federal level, IRS and Treasury's Office of Tax Policy provided new guidance for program stakeholders. At the state level, HFAs modified their QAPs for allocating tax credits.

IRS and Treasury Have Issued Guidance and Are Considering and Acting on Implementation Issues

HERA made changes to the LIHTC program that affected various parties, including taxpayers, HFAs, and project owners, and IRS and Treasury provided guidance and took other actions into 2012 to implement these changes. To better ensure that information on the HERA changes was widely accessible, IRS issued revenue procedures and notices, made changes to forms and form instructions, and circulated newsletters to program stakeholders.[19] More specifically, its actions included the following:

- Issuing (1) a revenue procedure for taxpayers to follow when choosing to no longer maintain a surety bond, as permitted by the HERA change described in table 2, item 6;[20] (2) a notice that the 9 percent floor (table 2, item 2) would apply to eligible projects that had committed to a lower rate before HERA; and (3) a newsletter to program stakeholders describing new income limits related to the HERA "hold harmless" provisions described in table 2, item 9. The income limits are a percentage of the relevant area's median gross

---

[19]A revenue procedure is an official statement of a procedure published in the Internal Revenue Bulletin that affects, for instance, the rights of a taxpayer under the Internal Revenue Code and should be a matter of public knowledge. It provides return filing or other instructions concerning an IRS position. A notice is a public pronouncement that may contain guidance involving substantive interpretation of the Code or other provisions of the law.

[20]A surety bond is a bond guaranteeing the performance of a contract or an obligation.

income and are the basis for calculating the gross rent that a LIHTC project can charge.[21]

- Updating instructions for Form 8609, "Low-Income Housing Credit Allocation and Certification," to reflect changes involving the 9 percent floor (table 2, item 2), federally subsidized buildings (table 2, item 4), and the HERA basis boost (table 2, item 3). HFAs use the form to report LIHTC allocations for buildings to IRS, and building owners use it to certify such things as a building's eligible basis, qualified basis, and placed-in-service date.

- Revising the *Guide for Completing Form 8823, Low-Income Housing Credit Agencies Report of Noncompliance or Building Disposition*, a guide intended to help housing agencies identify and consistently report noncompliance issues to IRS.

- Discussing through internal memorandums whether regulations needed to be updated because of HERA and exploring implementation issues that surfaced. For instance, IRS internally considered questions from the division tracking its own implementation of HERA's LIHTC provisions about whether the changes required updates to regulations governing general public use requirements mentioned in table 2, item 8. An official from IRS's Office of Chief Counsel told us they determined that no updates were needed.

Program stakeholders we spoke with, including HFAs, industry associations, syndicators, and developers, generally said that IRS's actions to implement the HERA changes were sufficient, and that they were satisfied with the agency's efforts. However, they raised two concerns in our discussions that IRS and Treasury have continued to consider and act on.

The first involved the HERA provision noted in table 2, item 5, that eased restrictions on using LIHTCs to acquire an existing building. Before

---

[21]For any project, the area median gross income determined for a particular year after 2008 is held harmless—it cannot be lower than the amount determined the year before. Also, for projects that had the area median gross income determined for 2007 or 2008, the area median gross income for years after 2008 is at least the amount at which HUD had held it harmless previously plus the amount by which the area median gross income increased after 2008.

HERA, acquisition costs for an existing building generally would not be eligible for LIHTCs unless the building had been placed in service 10 years or more before it was acquired. HERA waived this 10-year rule for any federally or state-assisted building—that is, any building that was "substantially" assisted, financed, or operated under certain federal or state programs or laws.

In response to this HERA provision, the IRS Chief Counsel and Treasury placed clarification of the meaning of "substantially" on priority lists of guidance projects for July 2010 through June 2011 and July 2011 through June 2012. With over 300 guidance projects on the priority list for 2011-2012, IRS and Treasury had not issued any guidance defining "substantially" as of October 2012. Agency officials cited the complexity of the issue and other agency priorities as reasons for the delay.[22] A Treasury official was not yet able to tell us when the agency would complete the guidance, what it was likely to say, or whether it would resolve the definition of "substantially" for both federal and state subsidies at the same time.

The relative importance of future guidance is unclear as stakeholders disagreed on the need to clarify the meaning of "substantially." Some stakeholders said there was little need for clarification. However, one organization sought guidance from Treasury in 2009 and 2010 because, it said, the lack of a definition was delaying some acquisition projects.[23] An IRS official agreed, saying the lack of guidance had delayed acquisition projects and resulted in the substitutions of other projects, such as construction of new buildings, for acquisitions. In addition, a Treasury official told us that the lack of guidance had likely made attorneys for potential LIHTC projects conservative in interpreting "substantially." For example, some may have decided that all the units in a building must be federally subsidized in order to meet the definition.

A second concern—related to HERA's hold harmless provisions on income and rent limits—did not rise to the level of necessarily requiring

---

[22]In previous reports, we have described delays in the priority guidance process. See GAO, *Tax Policy: The Research Tax Credit's Design and Administration Can Be Improved*, GAO-10-136 (Washington, D.C.: Nov. 6, 2009), and *Financial Derivatives: Disparate Tax Treatment and Information Gaps Create Uncertainty and Potential Abuse*, GAO-11-750 (Washington, D.C.: Sept. 20, 2011).

[23]The organization, the LIHTC Working Group, consists of LIHTC industry participants who work together to try to resolve technical and administrative LIHTC program issues.

formal guidance, but has received continued federal attention because of its complicated nature. The hold harmless provisions (table 2, item 9) are aimed at bolstering the financial viability of LIHTC projects by preventing rents from automatically falling when area income levels, on which the rents are based, decline. In so doing, the provisions resulted in a system in which, for instance, three projects on the same street could have three different sets of income and rent limits if they were placed in service in three different time periods. Accommodating all of the possibilities for different placed-in-service dates required projects to use multiple tables to find the applicable income and rent limits, and some program participants have found this confusing. Furthermore, the income and rent limits change annually when HUD publishes new area income levels. The owner of a LIHTC project must use the correct table, based on the building's location and placed-in-service date, to determine the maximum income that a household may have to be a qualified low-income household, and the maximum gross rent that a household may be charged, based on the number of bedrooms in the unit, for the unit to qualify for the credit as a low-income unit.

IRS issued explanatory newsletters about the hold harmless provisions, and IRS officials said they made public presentations to stakeholders about them, but some LIHTC program participants reported that the provisions were complicated, confusing, and hard to administer. For example, Texas HFA officials told us that the increase in the number of possible rent limits complicated communications with property owners and increased property owners' compliance risks. A Vermont HFA official described how staff had to learn to calculate new limits, publish and distribute new tables, and explain the changes in their QAP. However, some HFAs told us that while the provisions were complex and burdensome, they had worked hard to understand them and had learned to work with them. IRS has continued to provide explanatory newsletters and IRS officials told us they made public presentations into 2012. A Treasury official acknowledged the complexity of the provisions and said further clarifying guidance might be warranted. However, the official also said that making a change to hold harmless guidance would require determining that the change merited more consideration than the many non-HERA topics that Treasury also needed to consider.

HFAs Generally Implemented HERA Changes through Qualified Allocation Plans

HFAs we spoke with also took steps to implement the changes, including one of the changes HFAs generally thought was significant—the HERA basis boost. Our review of QAPs for nine HFAs and research by an industry group found that HFAs often modified their QAPs to implement the HERA basis boost but varied in how they used the new flexibility. Of the nine states we examined, eight modified their QAPs by revising their criteria for awarding the basis boost. According to a state official, the remaining HFA also revised its criteria for the basis boost but conveyed the changes to stakeholders through its website, public hearings, and newspapers.

In general, states varied in the criteria they developed for awarding the basis boost. We analyzed NCSHA summaries of the factors that HFAs reported considering in awarding the HERA basis boost in 2009, the first full year after HERA's enactment. According to the summaries, 30 of the 54 HFAs reporting cited specific factors beyond the single criterion given in HERA (financial feasibility).[24] The other 24 HFAs cited financial feasibility or other general guidance (17), did not report any factors (1), or chose not to implement the HERA basis boost (6). Research by NCSHA in 2010 noted that some states applied the boost statewide and some applied it to more specific geographical areas, project types, or projects with certain characteristics. NCSHA cited examples of states targeting the basis boost to developments that had tenants of different income levels, involved expensive land, were in rural or tribal areas or areas affected by natural disasters, featured "green building" practices or preservation initiatives, or were transit oriented.

States' use of the basis boost also varied over time. Our analysis of NCSHA summaries for 2008 through 2010 showed that HFAs' use of the HERA basis boost became more widespread over that period. More specifically, while 12 HFAs reported not having implemented the basis boost in 2008, this number dropped to 3 in 2010. For example, the Florida HFA did not begin to use the boost until the change appeared in its 2011 QAP because until then, the state was still benefitting from Gulf Opportunity Zone disaster credits and did not need the HERA basis boost.[25] California HFA officials said they did not use the boost as much as some other states because California already had a large number of counties that were designated as difficult development areas (DDA) and had a state LIHTC program covering projects that might have benefitted

---

[24]Although 56 HFAs receive LIHTC allocations, not all of them report information to NCSHA.

[25]Gulf Opportunity Zone disaster credits are LIHTCs, in addition to regular, annual allocations available to states, given to states affected by Gulf Coast hurricanes.

GAO-13-66 LIHTC Program Changes

from the HERA basis boost.[26] The officials said they did not use the HERA basis boost at all in 2012. The Massachusetts HFA began implementing the HERA basis boost in 2009 and continued to use it into 2012. In its 2009 plan, the HFA identified 20 locations that were eligible for the HERA basis boost, a number that rose to 35 in its 2012 plan.

HFAs also modified their QAPs and published technical information to reflect other program changes in HERA. For instance, soon after HERA was enacted, the Oregon HFA revised multiple sections of its QAP. In accordance with HERA changes, it added the historic nature of buildings and energy efficiency as criteria for awarding LIHTCs, updated policies on the availability of LIHTC projects for general public use, and inserted new policies on the use of the 9 percent floor. The Massachusetts HFA incorporated the increase in per capita allocations as well as the 9 percent floor into its 2008 QAP. In addition, some of the states we reviewed published technical information to help program stakeholders comply with HERA program changes. For example, as they had done in previous years, California HFA officials sent a memorandum to LIHTC project owners and applicants in December 2011 on revised rent and income limits the HFA had published, using information from HUD.

Available LIHTC Data Are Incomplete and Provide Limited Insight into Program Trends

HUD maintains a database of LIHTC-funded projects, which was last updated in July 2012, but the information it contains is incomplete. Although HUD has almost no direct administrative responsibility for the LIHTC program, as the federal government's lead housing agency, it has been voluntarily collecting information on the program since 1996 because of the importance of these credits as a source of funding for low-income housing. HUD's LIHTC Database, the largest source of federal information on the LIHTC program, aggregates project-level data that are voluntarily submitted by HFAs. HUD contracts with a consulting firm to help compile the database, which is updated annually and is available to the public on HUD's website.[27] Additionally, HUD sponsors studies of the LIHTC program that use these data. IRS, which jointly administers the program with HFAs, collects limited data that it needs to carry out its

---

[26]As previously noted, a DDA is any area designated by the Secretary of Housing and Urban Development as an area which has high construction, land, and utility costs relative to area median gross income.

[27]http://www.huduser.org/portal/datasets/lihtc.html.

mission of administering and enforcing the internal revenue laws.[28] It does not maintain the information needed to assess a housing production program, such as the types of tenants targeted and whether projects are in urban or rural areas.[29]

HUD's Database Is Incomplete Despite Efforts to Improve Data Collection

HUD's LIHTC Database does not capture all LIHTC projects placed in service, for three main reasons. First, although most HFAs voluntarily report LIHTC project data to HUD each year, some do not report consistently. Forty-two of 56 HFAs submitted project data to HUD for each year from 2006 through 2010. In 2010, these 42 HFAs received about 89 percent of all per capita LIHTC allocations. Of the remaining 14 HFAs, 2 did not report projects in any of the 5 years, while 12 did not report each year, but did report for at least 2 of the years. For these 12, all of the nonreporting was for 2008 through 2010 (the most recent reporting year), a period in which some HFAs were struggling to comply with a HERA requirement that they collect data on tenant characteristics (e.g., race and income) for LIHTC projects, according to HUD and NCSHA officials.[30]

The HERA provision containing this requirement authorized $6.1 million for fiscal years 2009 through 2013 for HUD to, among other things, provide technical assistance to HFAs and compile the tenant data, but HUD never received any appropriations for these tasks. HUD is working to fulfill the requirement with existing resources. For example, HUD streamlined the project and tenant data collections by merging the two

---

[28]The lack of data is fairly typical with tax expenditures such as the LIHTC program. Tax expenditures are reductions in a taxpayer's tax liability that result from special credits, deductions, exemptions and exclusions from taxation, deferral of tax liability, and preferential tax rates. We previously reported that even basic information about who claims tax benefits and which communities benefit from specific activities from tax expenditures is often lacking. As a result, information often has not been available to help Congress determine the effectiveness of some tax expenditures. For more information, see GAO, *Tax Policy: Factors for Evaluating Expiring Tax Provisions,* GAO-12-760T (Washington, D.C.: June 8, 2012) and *Community Development: Limited Information on the Use and Effectiveness of Tax Expenditures Could Be Mitigated through Congressional Attention,* GAO-12-262 (Washington, D.C.: Feb. 29, 2012).

[29]A private accounting firm has also collected LIHTC project information, including information on project characteristics, by surveying LIHTC investors and syndicators. However, this database also does not capture all LIHTC projects, and is not publicly available.

[30]HERA at § 2835(d). Pub. L. No. 110-289 (codified at 42 U.S.C. § 1437z-8).

efforts. It also required HFAs to submit data in a standardized electronic format via a secure web portal. According to HUD, this change is significant, as the prior data collection process involved a HUD contractor that contacted each HFA and then standardized the collected data, which HFAs often maintained in different formats. HUD said that although some HFAs would need several years to make the transition, the new system was the most cost-effective long-term solution. HUD also said it recognized the problem of underreporting in recent years but that until the transition to the new data collection method was completed, its options were to either knowingly underreport properties placed in service or not release any data for those years.

Second, in recent years, HUD has not identified or followed up on cases in which HFAs reported a substantially lower number of projects than in past years, although such information could potentially be incomplete. For example, HUD's database showed that one state had between 23 and 49 projects placed in service each year from 2006 through 2009, but only 2 projects in 2010. When we followed up with the HFA in this state, HFA officials provided us with documentation showing that they had reported 37 projects for 2010. Similarly, HUD's database showed that another state had 2 projects placed in service in 2008, compared with 90 or more in each of the 2 previous years. An official from this state's HFA told us that the actual number for 2008 was 96 properties. We provided HUD with these and other examples for their review. According to a HUD official, before 2008 its contractor followed up with HFAs on these types of data anomalies but now places less emphasis on this function because of resource limitations and the HERA requirement for tenant data. Instead, the contractor now focuses on assisting HFAs with meeting the tenant data requirement and follows up only with HFAs that do not report any project data at all.

Third, at the time they reported to HUD, HFAs may not have had information on all projects placed in service. Specifically, HFA officials said that delays between the date when a project was placed in service, the date a project owner reported it to the HFA, and the date the HFA recorded it in its information system could result in underreporting of projects. HUD instructs states to review the property information previously submitted and include information for these omitted properties. As a result, these omissions may be corrected in subsequent data submissions.

Even when HUD did receive project data, much of it was incomplete, omitting information on project characteristics such as the type of location, construction, and tenants targeted. The proportion of missing information on project characteristics increased after 2007 (see table 3). For example, the proportion of missing information on the types of tenants targeted increased from 5 percent in 2006 to 28 percent in 2010. A HUD official noted that the HERA provision requiring HFAs to collect data on the characteristics of tenants in LIHTC projects had made it more challenging for HFAs to also report the project data with existing resources. In addition, a HUD official explained that across HFAs, different offices maintain tenant-level and project-level data. He said that HUD's data request was often completed by the offices with the tenant data, which might not have detailed project information. The official added that he had emphasized the need for HFAs to direct HUD's request for project data to the appropriate office in presentations to an HFA association and in communications with individual HFAs. However, according to HUD, resource limitations have prevented HUD and its contractor from performing thorough follow up with HFAs about missing information on project characteristics.

Table 3: Percentage of Projects with Missing Information by Project Characteristics, Calendar Years 2006-2010, as of July 2012

Project characteristic	Percentage of projects with missing information by year placed in service				
	2006	2007	2008	2009	2010
Location type (e.g., metropolitan, nonmetropolitan)	10%	8%	11%	14%	17%
Construction type (e.g., new construction, acquisition and rehabilitation)	5%	5%	10%	12%	17%
Types of tenants targeted (e.g., elderly, family, disabled)	5%	8%	17%	23%	28%

Source: GAO analysis of HUD's L HTC Database.

Note: Data are for the 42 HFAs that reported information on LIHTC projects each year from 2006 through 2010.

Having complete data on the LIHTC program is important because of the program's significance to overall federal efforts to meet the nation's affordable housing needs. As previously noted, the LIHTC program is the largest subsidy program for constructing and rehabilitating low-income rental housing. Additionally, the program is used in conjunction with other federal housing programs, including HUD's programs. For example, some LIHTC projects receive grants through HUD's HOME Investment Partnership program and have mortgages that are insured by HUD's

Federal Housing Administration.[31] HUD's LIHTC Database is the federal government's main source of information on LIHTC projects, and HUD and others have used data from 2007 and earlier—prior to some of the challenges discussed previously—to conduct research on the LIHTC program. For example, one study HUD sponsored examined the geographic distribution of LIHTC projects to assess whether program rules contribute to clustering of subsidized housing in central city and high-poverty areas.[32] Another HUD-sponsored study examined whether LIHTC projects continue to provide affordable housing after the 15-year period in which they are required to do so.[33] In addition, the Rental Policy Working Group established by the White House's Domestic Policy Council has used the data to examine the potential for harmonizing and streamlining property inspection requirements for rental properties with multiple sources of federal funding, including LIHTCs.[34] However, as we have seen, a number of challenges faced by HUD and HFAs have adversely affected the completeness of HUD's database. Without more complete data on the number, location, and characteristics of LIHTC projects, the federal government's ability to continue evaluating program outcomes and overall federal efforts to provide affordable housing is limited.

---

[31]HOME is the largest federal program that awards block grants to state and local governments exclusively to create affordable housing for low-income households.

[32]Casey J. Dawkins, *Exploring the Spatial Distribution of Low-Income Housing Tax Credit Properties*, Assisted Housing Research Cadre Report, prepared for the Department of Housing and Urban Development, Office of Policy and Development Research (Washington, D.C.: February 2011).

[33]Jill Khadduri, Carissa Climaco, Kimberly Burnett, Laurie Gould, and Louise Elving, *What Happens to Low-Income Housing Tax Credit Properties at Year 15 and Beyond?* Report prepared for the Department of Housing and Urban Development by Abt Associates, in partnership with VIVA Consulting (Washington, D.C.: August 2012).

[34]The working group consists of the White House Domestic Policy Council, National Economic Council, Office of Management and Budget, HUD, U.S. Department of Agriculture, and Treasury. The purpose of the working group is to better align rental requirements across programs, and thereby increase the effectiveness of federal rental policy and improve participant outcomes.

Available Data Provide Limited Insight into Trends in the Number and Characteristics of LIHTC Projects

According to HUD data as of July 2012, the 42 HFAs that submitted information for each year from 2006 through 2010 reported that more than 5,300 LIHTC projects were placed in service over the 5-year period (see table 4).[35] In total, these projects used more than $3 billion in LIHTCs and contained more than 421,000 living units. The reported number of projects and units placed in service declined over the 5-year period, particularly after 2008; however, the lack of complete project data, as discussed previously, prevents a reliable analysis of actual program trends.

Table 4: Reported Number of LIHTC Projects Placed in Service, Calendar Years 2006-2010, as of July 2012

	2006	2007	2008	2009	2010	Total
Number of projects placed in service	1,387	1,286	1,225	886	594	5,378
Number of units placed in service	112,612	100,980	86,283	65,409	56,265	421,549
Amount of LIHTCs used for projects placed in service	$664,950,647	$661,318,390	$686,848,400	$568,352,441	$454,559,496	$3,036,029,374

Source: GAO analysis of HUD's LIHTC Database.

Note: Data are for the 42 HFAs that reported information on LIHTC projects each year from 2006 through 2010. The lack of complete project data prevents a reliable analysis of program trends.

Although data at the national level are limited, information from the nine HFAs we contacted provide some insight into changes in the number of projects placed in service after HERA was enacted in 2008. Six of the nine HFAs indicated that the number of projects declined substantially between 2008 and 2009, while the other three experienced either modest or no declines. For example, California HFA officials said they had 203 projects placed in service in 2008, compared with 140 in 2009. In contrast, Massachusetts HFA officials said they had 21 projects placed in service in both years. Of the six HFAs that had substantial declines, three continued to see decreases in 2010, while the remainder experienced modest to large increases in 2010.[36]

While a portion of LIHTC projects in HUD's database lack information on location type, the data do indicate that the majority of LIHTC projects

---

[35]LIHTC projects are generally placed in service 1 to 2 years after receiving tax credit allocations. For example, projects placed in service in 2010 likely received allocations in 2008 or 2009.

[36]As discussed in the next section of this report, some of the unused credits were exchanged for cash grants or reallocated to future projects.

placed in service from 2006 through 2010 were located in metropolitan central and noncentral cities (e.g., suburbs). For each of these years, at least 69 percent of reported projects were in metropolitan areas, but given the proportion of projects with missing information on location type, trends in this characteristic cannot be precisely determined (see table 5).

Table 5: Percentage of Reported LIHTC Projects Placed in Service from Calendar Years 2006-2010 by Location Type, as of July 2012

| Location type | Percentage of projects by year placed in service | | | | |
	2006	2007	2008	2009	2010
Metropolitan/central city	42%	47%	40%	45%	43%
Metropolitan/noncentral city	27%	24%	30%	25%	27%
Nonmetropolitan	21%	21%	19%	16%	13%
Location type not indicated	10%	8%	11%	14%	17%

Source: GAO analysis of HUD's L HTC Database.

Note: Data are for the 42 HFAs that reported information on LIHTC projects each year from 2006 through 2010.

According to HUD data, the majority of reported LIHTC projects placed in service from 2006 through 2010 were newly constructed (see table 6). However, the amount of missing data on construction type after 2007 makes it impossible to draw accurate conclusions on potential changes in the proportion of projects that were newly constructed and those that were acquisition and rehabilitation projects.

Table 6: Percentage of Reported LIHTC Projects by Construction Type, Calendar Years 2006-2010, as of July 2012

| Construction type | Percentage of projects by year placed in service | | | | |
	2006	2007	2008	2009	2010
New construction	58%	59%	55%	55%	54%
Acquisition and rehabilitation	33%	33%	31%	31%	27%
Both new construction and acquisition/rehabilitation	2%	1%	2%	1%	1%
Missing construction type	5%	5%	10%	12%	17%

Source: GAO analysis of HUD's L HTC Database.

Note: Data are for the 42 HFAs that reported information on LIHTC projects each year from 2006 through 2010. Columns may not sum to 100 percent due to rounding.

According to data reported to HUD, the most common types of tenants targeted by LIHTC projects in 2006 and 2007 were families and elderly tenants (see table 7). However, as previously noted, the proportion of projects in HUD's database with missing information on tenant types increased substantially after 2007. As a result, any reported changes in types of tenants targeted are not definitive. In addition, HUD officials told us that HFAs may have used different criteria for determining whether a project was targeted to particular groups of tenants, potentially resulting in inconsistencies across HFAs.

Table 7: Percentage of Reported LIHTC Projects by Type of Tenant Targeted, 2006-2010, as of July 2012

Tenants targeted	Percentage of projects by year placed in service				
	2006	2007	2008	2009	2010
Family	45%	42%	44%	38%	30%
Elderly	24%	25%	23%	20%	21%
Disabled	9%	10%	15%	12%	15%
Homeless	3%	4%	8%	7%	7%
Other	6%	10%	7%	10%	7%
Did not target	22%	20%	14%	13%	14%
Not indicated	5%	8%	17%	23%	28%

Source: GAO analysis of HUD's National L HTC Database.

Notes: Percentages may sum to more than 100 percent because projects can target more than one type of tenant. Data are for 42 HFAs that reported LIHTC projects to HUD in each of these years.

Stakeholders Said HERA Provisions Helped the Financial Feasibility of Some LIHTC Projects

State and industry officials we spoke with said that isolating the effect of the HERA changes on the overall LIHTC market was difficult because of other program changes (e.g., creation of the Exchange Program) and economic developments (e.g., the recession and financial crisis) that occurred around the same time. Nonetheless, state and industry officials we spoke with identified specific LIHTC projects that they said would not have been completed without certain HERA provisions. In particular, they cited the temporary increase in per capita credit allocations, the temporary 9 percent floor, and the HERA basis boost as three provisions that helped the financial feasibility of some projects and likely prevented even further decreases in LIHTC projects after 2008. In addition, stakeholders said HERA changes particularly helped the financial feasibility of rural projects.

Stakeholders Identified HERA Changes That Enhanced Project Feasibility

Temporary Increase in Per Capita Credits

Because of HERA's temporary increase in per capita credit allocations, HFAs received tens of millions of dollars more in allocations in 2008 and 2009 than they would have otherwise. By statute, LIHTC allocation amounts are adjusted for inflation each calendar year, but for calendar years 2008 and 2009 only, HERA further increased allocations to each HFA. Adjusted for inflation, the per capita allocation in 2008 would have been $2.00, but HERA increased the amount to $2.20 that year and to $2.30 in 2009. The minimum allocation for small HFAs was increased to $2,555,000 in 2008 and $2,665,000 in 2009. Without HERA, HFAs would have received $61,836,050 less in per capita credits than they did in 2008 and $62,408,937 less in 2009. For 2010, LIHTC allocations returned to the path that would have been in place if HERA had not been enacted (see table 8).

Table 8: Per Capita LIHTC Allocations, Calendar Years 2006-2010, Including HERA Increases in 2008 and 2009

Calendar year	Credit per capita	Total per capita credits	Percentage change in total credits from previous year
2006	$1.90	$575,565,080	---
2007	$1.95	$598,946,906	4.06
2008	$2.20	$680,421,802	13.60
2009	$2.30	$716,847,811	5.35
2010	$2.10	$662,928,791	-7.52

Source: GAO analysis of data from NCSHA and RS.

Some state officials we spoke with said that they allocated the additional credits to projects already under development and to new projects. For example, HFA officials in Michigan and Oregon told us that they used the additional credits to both fill funding gaps for projects that had previously received LIHTC allocations and to fund one or two additional projects in their states. Massachusetts HFA officials told us that they used the additional credits to finish projects that were in danger of not being completed because of drops in prices that investors were willing to pay for LIHTCs.

Although HFAs received additional credits in 2008 and 2009, developers also returned more unused credits to HFAs in these years. According to data from NCSHA, the total amount of credits developers returned to HFAs increased substantially in 2008 and 2009. The amount of returned credits in 2009 was more than 6 times the amount in 2006 (see table 9).

Table 9: Amount of Credits Developers Returned to HFAs, Calendar Years 2006-2010

Calendar year	Credits developers returned to HFAs
2006	$66,809,433
2007	$68,641,795
2008	$108,431,328
2009	$426,862,481
2010	$72,322,543

Source: GAO analysis of data from NCSHA.

An NCSHA official explained that developers returned credits for several reasons. For example, the NCSHA official noted that in 2008, developers had trouble finding LIHTC investors, resulting in a higher-than-normal amount returned to the HFAs. Also, in 2009, the Recovery Act's Exchange Program allowed HFAs to exchange returned credits for cash grants, resulting in a very high amount of returns that year. For 2009, the amount of returned credits included those that were returned and exchanged, as well as those returned and possibly reallocated to other developers. According to the NCSHA official, virtually all of the returned credits that were not exchanged were reallocated either the same year or the following year.

Temporary 9 Percent Floor and Basis Boost

Some state housing officials and industry stakeholders said that HERA's temporary floor for the 9 percent credit helped the financial feasibility of individual projects. Owing to the floating credit rate prior to HERA, developers that received the 9 percent credit actually received a credit approximating 8 percent. By setting a floor of 9 percent for projects placed in service by the end of 2013, HERA increased the amount of credits these projects could receive. For example, if a pre-HERA project had an eligible basis of $1,000,000 and the floating rate for the 9 percent credit was 8 percent, that project would be eligible to receive $800,000 in credits ($80,000 per year for 10 years). In contrast, by setting a floor of 9 percent for the 9 percent credit, that same project would be eligible for $900,000 in credits ($90,000 per year for 10 years).

Also, as previously noted, the HERA basis boost provision gave HFAs the ability to designate any building, regardless of location, as eligible for an enhanced credit of up to 130 percent of the building's eligible basis rather than just those in a DDA or a QCT. One developer told us that every LIHTC project he had completed since the passage of HERA used the HERA basis boost, and that it and the 9 percent floor together had made a significant difference in his ability to complete projects. This developer cited a project in which these two provisions reduced a funding gap of $1,680,000 to $450,000, which the developer was able to close by other means. Another LIHTC developer noted that the 9 percent floor allowed LIHTC deals to be engineered with fewer funding sources and that in many cases such deals would not have been completed without this provision. In addition, North Carolina HFA officials told us that some projects had received tax credit awards in 2007 and 2008, but had funding gaps when the tax credit market collapsed and prices for tax credits fell before developers could secure equity from investors. For these projects, the HFA allowed developers to return their allocated credits and receive new credits with the 9 percent rate and the HERA basis boost, thus filling the funding gaps. According to the North Carolina officials, these HERA provisions helped in completing a total of 46 projects that likely would not otherwise have been completed.

In addition, HFA officials in Oregon and Michigan noted that they used the HERA basis boost for permanent supportive housing—long-term housing projects with supportive services for homeless persons with disabilities or other barriers—which have lower income tenants. Similarly, HFA officials in Florida said that the HERA basis boost helped fund three projects that will be placed in service in either 2012 or 2013 for tenants that were homeless and had lower incomes. According to the officials, such projects are typically difficult to develop because project cash flows are limited because tenants may not have any income when they move in. HFA officials in Minnesota said that without the 9 percent floor, it would have been difficult to fund projects serving the long-term homeless, those with special needs, and those with lower incomes.

Stakeholders Said HERA Changes Helped Rural Projects

According to state housing officials and industry participants, certain HERA provisions helped mitigate some of the challenges associated with developing projects in rural areas. For example, the maximum amount of rent a project owner can charge is based on the area's income limits. According to officials from the Council for Affordable and Rural Housing, because rural areas often have lower income limits compared with urban areas, rural projects also often have lower cash flows from rents. They noted that the HERA provision that allowed projects in rural areas to base tenant income limits on the greater of the area median gross income or the national nonmetropolitan median gross income was one of the most significant HERA provisions for rural housing. In cases where the national nonmetropolitan measure is greater than the local area measure, project owners can set higher rent levels than they would have prior to HERA. This flexibility, in turn, can give project owners access to a broader pool of qualified tenants and increase cash flows from rent, potentially making the projects more attractive to investors. Additionally, according to some industry stakeholders, investor demand for LIHTCs is often weaker in rural areas than in urban areas in part because rural LIHTC projects tend to be smaller in scale. As a result, fixed transaction costs are spread over fewer units, and a few vacancies can have a relatively greater impact on the viability of a small project. Some state officials told us they applied the HERA basis boost to rural areas to help strengthen the financial viability of projects in these locations. For example, Michigan HFA officials said they applied the HERA basis boost to rural areas because rural projects would not have been desirable to investors without it.

Conclusions

The LIHTC program is the largest federal program for building and rehabilitating affordable rental housing and provides billions of dollars in tax credits each year. Through HERA, Congress made a number of changes to the program and sought analysis of credit allocations made before and after the act's implementation. However, limitations in available program data hamper this type of analysis and potentially other research that could be useful to policymakers. HUD is not required to collect data on LIHTC projects and has very limited administrative responsibility for the program, but it has collected some information from HFAs for many years. We commend HUD for taking steps as the lead federal housing agency to collect and disseminate project information. This information has been used to examine important issues, such as the extent to which subsidized housing remains affordable over the long term and the potential for harmonizing requirements across federal housing programs. But, in recent years, the completeness of HUD's LIHTC Database has worsened, due partly to resource constraints and challenges HUD and HFAs face in meeting new requirements for compiling information on tenants in LIHTC projects. In addition, HUD and its contractor have not followed up on data anomalies that could indicate incomplete reporting. Our work suggests that HUD's database may be missing many projects that could be captured through additional follow-up efforts. Without improvements in the database, the federal government's ability to evaluate basic program outcomes—such as how much housing was produced—and other aspects of federal housing policy may suffer.

Recommendation for Executive Action

HUD has taken steps to improve its data collection process and faces resource constraints. However, the importance of the LIHTC program to federal housing policy underscores the need for continued attention to data quality and completeness. Therefore, we recommend that the Secretary of Housing and Urban Development (1) evaluate options for improving the completeness of HUD's LIHTC Database, including following up on data anomalies and enhancing the role of HUD's contractor in data collection and quality control; and (2) based on this evaluation, take additional steps to improve the data.

Agency Comments and Our Evaluation

We provided a draft of this report to HUD, IRS, and Treasury for their review and comment. We received written comments from HUD's Acting Assistant Secretary for Policy Development and Research that are reprinted in appendix III. We also received technical comments from IRS and Treasury, which we incorporated into the final report where appropriate.

In its written comments, HUD agreed with our conclusions and recommendations but expressed concerns about the draft report's characterization of HUD's LIHTC Database and data collection efforts. HUD said that our draft report did not adequately explain either the transition HUD was experiencing in its data collection or changes it had made to the collection process. HUD noted, as did our draft report, that while HERA required the agency to compile data on tenants in LIHTC units and authorized $6.1 million for this purpose, Congress did not appropriate these funds. HUD stated that to more cost-effectively collect both the tenant and property data, it merged the two efforts and required HFAs to submit all of the data through a secure web portal in a standardized electronic format. HUD said that it understood that this requirement would entail a multiyear transition for some HFAs, but also noted that in the long run this solution was the most cost-effective way to collect the information. Additionally, HUD said it recognized that its database had suffered from underreporting in recent years but said that until the transition to the new data collection method was completed, its options were either to knowingly underreport properties placed in service or to not release any data for those years. In response to HUD's comments, we added language to the final report clarifying the connection between resource constraints for the implementation of the tenant data requirement and the completeness of the project data. We also added language describing how HUD had modified its data collection process and its rationale for reporting incomplete data rather than no data.

HUD also expressed concern about our use of the word "inaccurate" to describe potential shortcomings in some of the information in the LIHTC Database. HUD said that it would never publicly release information that it thought might be inaccurate and suggested that we substitute "incomplete" for "inaccurate." Our draft report generally used the word "incomplete" to characterize the information in the LIHTC Database but in three places used the phrase "potentially inaccurate information" to describe cases in which the LIHTC Database showed substantially fewer projects for an HFA than the number we obtained from the HFA directly. We agree that "incomplete" is a more appropriate term and revised the final report to use that word throughout.

We are sending copies of this report to interested congressional committees, the Secretary of the Treasury, the Commissioner of Internal Revenue, and the Secretary of Housing and Urban Development. This report is also available at no charge on the GAO website at http://www.gao.gov.

If you or your staffs have any questions about this report, please contact us at (202) 512-8678 or garciadiazd@gao.gov, or (202) 512-9110 or whitej@gao.gov. Contact points for our Offices of Congressional Relations and Public Affairs may be found on the last page of this report. GAO staff who made major contributions to this report are listed in appendix IV.

Daniel Garcia-Diaz
Acting Director
Financial Markets and Community Investment

James R. White
Director
Strategic Issues

Appendix I: Objectives, Scope, and Methodology

This report discusses (1) how the Internal Revenue Service (IRS) and selected housing finance agencies (HFA) implemented the Housing and Economic Recovery Act of 2008 (HERA) changes to the Low-Income Housing Tax Credit (LIHTC) program, (2) what the Department of Housing and Urban Development's (HUD) data on LIHTC projects show about the number and characteristics of projects completed from 2006 through 2010 and any data limitations, and (3) the views of program stakeholders about the effects of the HERA changes on these projects.

To assess how IRS and selected HFAs implemented HERA changes to the LIHTC program, we reviewed IRS guidance, memorandums, and planning documents. We also interviewed IRS and Department of the Treasury officials. In addition, we interviewed officials from nine HFAs: California, Florida, Massachusetts, Michigan, Minnesota, North Carolina, Oregon, Texas, and Vermont. We selected these HFAs to cover different regions of the country and amounts of tax credit allocations. The selected states are not representative of the entire LIHTC market. For the selected HFAs, we reviewed qualified allocation plans (QAP) that contained detailed selection criteria and application requirements for LIHTCs. To further learn how HERA changes were implemented, we interviewed other industry stakeholders, such as industry associations, investors, syndicators, and housing developers.

To examine HUD's data on LIHTC projects and what these data show about the number and characteristics of LIHTC projects completed from 2006 through 2010, we analyzed information from HUD's LIHTC Database.[1] HUD collects these data from HFAs and maintains information on LIHTC-financed projects once they are placed in service. We conducted reasonableness checks on the data to identify any missing, erroneous, or outlying figures. We also asked the nine HFAs previously mentioned to check HUD's numbers of projects placed in service from 2006 through 2010 against their own records, and interviewed HUD about how it and its contractor compiled the data. As discussed in the body of this report, we found that HUD's data may not contain all LIHTC projects placed in service as of 2010 for several reasons, including (1) challenges states face in implementing new requirements for reporting tenant data and (2) delays between when a project is placed in service and when that information is entered into the

---

[1]The most recent data available from the database are for properties placed in service in 2010.

state's data system and reported to HUD. As a result, the number of reported projects placed in service as of 2010 may be understated. We also found that a substantial proportion of projects in the database had missing values for key project characteristics. For this reason, changes in the reported number and characteristics of projects over time should be interpreted with caution. While we acknowledge these limitations, we chose to present the LIHTC data as reported by HUD because they provided the broadest coverage of LIHTC projects placed in service through 2010. We concluded that the data elements we used were sufficiently reliable for describing limitations of the data and presenting the project information HUD had compiled as of July 2012. For each year, we totaled the number of projects placed in service. Due to the limitations of HUD's data, we supplemented this analysis by examining information from the nine HFAs we contacted to identify any state-level trends. Using the HUD data, we calculated the proportion of projects with certain characteristics, including location type (metropolitan/central city, metropolitan noncentral city, nonmetropolitan), construction type (new construction, acquisition/rehabilitation, both new construction and acquisition/rehabilitation), and the type of tenants targeted (elderly, family, disabled, homeless, other). In addition, because HERA increased the amount of credits allocated to states in 2008 and 2009, we analyzed trends in annual LIHTC allocations from 2006 through 2010 using data collected by the National Council of State Housing Agencies (NCSHA). In order to assess the reliability of the NCSHA data we analyzed, we reviewed documentation and interviewed NCHSA officials about their methods for collecting and reporting the data. We concluded that the NCHSA data were sufficiently reliable for our purposes.

To obtain the views of selected HFAs and industry participants about the effects of the HERA changes on LIHTC projects, we interviewed officials from the HFAs and industry stakeholders noted previously. We obtained their views on which HERA changes were most significant, the extent to which the HERA changes helped complete projects that otherwise would not have been feasible, and the extent to which the HERA changes affected the characteristics of projects that received LIHTC allocations. In addition, we reviewed documentation on projects that industry stakeholders said had been affected by the changes.

We conducted this performance audit from February through December 2012 in accordance with generally accepted government auditing standards. Those standards require that we plan and perform the audit to obtain sufficient, appropriate evidence to provide a reasonable basis for our findings and conclusions based on our audit objectives. We believe

that the evidence obtained provides a reasonable basis for our findings
and conclusions based on our audit objectives.

Appendix II: Specific 2008 Changes Related to the Low-Income Housing Tax Credit

Table 10 summarizes the changes related to the LIHTC program made in the Multi-Family Housing subtitle of HERA.[1]

Table 10: Specific LIHTC Provisions Enacted in 2008, by Category

Temporary increase in per capita credit allocations to states

- For 2008 and 2009 only, increased the per-resident credit amount a state may allocate and the small-state minimum annual cap

Determination of credit rate

- For buildings placed in service after July 30, 2008, and before December 31, 2013, established a 9 percent minimum credit rate for newly constructed and substantially rehabilitated nonfederally subsidized buildings
- Redefined the criteria for considering whether a building is federally subsidized by not counting certain federal loans and assistance

Changes to definition of eligible basis

- Gave states the flexibility to designate buildings as eligible for an enhanced credit of 130 percent of the normal amount when the buildings needed the enhanced credit in order to be financially feasible
- Increased the minimum rehabilitation expenses needed for existing buildings to be eligible for the credit
- Expanded the size of the community service facility that is counted as part of the eligible basis of a low-income building
- Clarified how federal grants are treated in reducing a building's eligible basis
- Redefined related persons to include only those with a 50 percent ownership commonality (raised from 10 percent)
- Expanded the definition of a federally assisted building and included state-assisted buildings in the waiver of the 10-year rule on change of ownership

Other simplification and reform of low-income housing tax incentives

- Repealed prohibition on the credit for buildings receiving HUD moderate rehabilitation help
- Gave projects 1 year, not 6 months, after credit allocation to incur 10 percent of reasonably expected costs
- For buildings disposed of, released the disposition bond requirement to avoid recapture
- Added energy-efficiency and "historic nature" criteria to criteria that states must set forth in qualified allocation plans
- Added an exception to a general rule prohibiting 100 percent full-time student households from occupying low-income units to allow a unit occupied by a student who had previously received foster care to be eligible for the credit
- Changed median income rules in rural areas
- Clarified a provision so that a project would not fail the general public use requirement just because it favored tenants who had special needs, were members of specified groups, or were involved in artistic or literary activities

Treatment of basic housing allowances

- Excluded military basic housing allowances from income for purposes of income eligibility rules in certain locations

Refunding treatment for certain multifamily housing bonds

- Treated a bond issued to refinance a first issue of bonds as a refunding issue

---

[1]Pub. L. No. 110-289, div. C, title I, subtitle A, 122 Stat. 2878-2888 (July 30, 2008).

Coordination of certain tax-exempt bond rules and credit rules

- Conformed rules so that in both cases certain restrictions will be satisfied if the next available unit in a building is rented to a new tenant who satisfies income and rent-restriction requirements
- Conformed rules related to residential units occupied by 100 percent low-income student households
- Conformed rules related to single-room occupancy housing

Hold harmless for reductions in area median gross income

- Changed how area median gross income is determined

Exception from annual recertification requirement

- For projects that are 100 percent low income, waived the requirement for annual tenant income recertifications

Source: GAO analysis of Joint Committee on Taxation, *General Explanation of Tax Legislation Enacted in the 110th Congress*, JCS-1-09 (March 2009).

Appendix III: Comments from the Department of Housing and Urban Development

U.S. DEPARTMENT OF HOUSING AND URBAN DEVELOPMENT
WASHINGTON, DC 20410-6000

ASSISTANT SECRETARY FOR
POLICY DEVELOPMENT AND RESEARCH

NOV 2 8 2012

Mr. Daniel Garcia-Diaz
 Mr. James R. White
U.S. Government Accountability Office (GAO)
441 G Street NW
Washington, DC 20548-0001

Dear Mr. Diaz and Mr. White:

Thank you for providing the Department of Housing and Urban Development's Office of Policy Development and Research (PD&R) the opportunity to review the draft report, "Low-Income Housing Tax Credits: Agencies Implemented Changes Enacted in 2008, but Project Data Collection Could be Improved." As you know, PD&R staff provided considerable guidance and assistance for the report on PD&R's Low-Income Housing Tax Credit (LIHTC) properties placed in service database. However, after reviewing the report, HUD finds there are several important omissions and mischaracterizations that distract from the purpose of the report and that could significantly undermine PD&R's efforts to collect and report data on a housing production program over which it has no administrative authority. HUD's concerns are explained below and the Department would appreciate GAO's attention and response to them in the final report.

Most importantly, pages 17 through 23 of the draft report could be improved to better describe the current state of PD&R's database and the many efforts HUD has taken to efficiently carry-out the data collection efforts. As the GAO research team knows, PD&R began collecting the property data in the mid-1990s because of the lack of a consistent source of LIHTC program data on a national basis. Since HUD does not have a direct role in the administration of this program and the Internal Revenue Service (IRS) does not release any of its information on LIHTC properties, the data is collected from the sixty state and local housing finance agencies (HFAs) that administer the program. Many of these agencies have limited staff time to devote to responding to HUD's data request. In order to compensate for their lack of capacity, HUD chose to use its own resources and fund a contractor who worked closely with the HFAs to ensure complete, accurate and consistent reporting. Until the passage of HERA in 2008, PD&R's LIHTC database was generally complete and regarded as the most comprehensive, if not the only, national source of LIHTC property data, and was used widely in independent academic studies of the LIHTC program (for recent examples, see: Nathaniel Baum-Snow and Justin Marion, 2009, "The Effects of Low-Income Housing Tax Credit Developments on Neighborhoods," Journal of Public Economics, 93: 655-666; and Michael D. Eriksen, and Stuart S. Rosenthal, 2010, "Crowd Out Effects of Place-Based Subsidized Rental Housing: New Evidence from the LIHTC Program," Journal of Public Economics, 94: 953-66).

www.hud.gov   espanol.hud.gov

2

The passage of HERA in 2008, specifically its mandate that the state HFAs provide HUD demographic and economic data on tenants in LIHTC units, required PD&R to significantly modify its well-established methodology for collecting LIHTC property information. As GAO mentions in the draft report, HERA authorized $6.1 million over five years to fund the submission of LIHTC tenant data from the state HFAs to HUD. These funds were to support not only IT infrastructure within HUD, but also to provide funds to the HFAs to upgrade their LIHTC program administrative data systems, which for many states did not even exist. Unfortunately, Congress did not appropriate any funds to support this mandate. Despite the lack of specific appropriated funds, HUD decided to carry-out Congress' mandate using its existing resources. The most cost effective way to collect data, regardless of whether the authorized funding was appropriated, was to merge the property and tenant data collections, since both sets of data were provided by the same set of state and local agencies. In 2010, using industry-accepted and endorsed standards of electronic data submission, HUD required that all property, and tenant, data be submitted through a secure portal on HUDUser.org in an XML formatted file. The requirement that the data be submitted in a specific, electronic format was a stark change in the collection methodology, and one that PD&R understood would entail a multi-year transition for some agencies, but it was indeed the most cost effective solution for the long-run viability of HUD's LIHTC data collection responsibilities.

HUD is concerned because the draft report: 1) does not adequately explain the transition that the data collection is experiencing, due to HERA, and 2) does not explain the steps HUD has taken to make the process of collecting LIHTC project data more cost-effective. PD&R acknowledges that the database has suffered from under-reporting over the past few years and is taking steps, beyond the change in collection methodology described above, to improve the data coverage. While the Department completes the transition to the more cost-effective methodology given the shortage of funds, PD&R's options are to either knowingly under-report properties placed into service, or not release any data for these years. PD&R has chosen to release the partial, but not inaccurate, data with the proper caveats noted on HUDUser.org, where the database is available.

In the discussion of HUD's database in the draft report, GAO states that the database contains, or may contain, "inaccurate" information and, even worse, that HUD is aware that the database contains inaccurate information. I believe what GAO truly means is "incomplete" rather than "inaccurate." HUD would never publically release information that it thought may be inaccurate and in fact, GAO staff did not identify any information that was potentially inaccurate, but rather found, as acknowledged by HUD staff, that the information, specifically the number of properties placed into service through 2010, was incomplete at the time the GAO accessed the data.

3

The Department agrees with the conclusions and recommendations in the draft report that HUD should continue evaluating ways to improve the data collection on an on-going basis so that the LIHTC database can be more complete in a timelier manner.

The Department looks forward to seeing GAO's response to HUD's concerns in the final report. The report is an important contribution to understanding the LIHTC program, which is why HUD is invested in ensuring its role is accurately described. Please let me know if I can provide any additional information.

Sincerely,

Erika C. Poethig
Acting Assistant Secretary for Policy
Development and Research

Appendix IV: GAO Contacts and Staff Acknowledgments

GAO Contacts	Daniel Garcia-Diaz, (202) 512-8678 or garciadiazd@gao.gov
	James R. White, (202) 512-9110 or whitej@gao.gov
Staff Acknowledgments	In addition to the contacts named above, Steve Westley and Joanna Stamatiades (Assistant Directors), Emily Chalmers, William Chatlos, Lois Hanshaw, Lawrence Korb, May Lee, John McGrail, Marc Molino, Edward Nannenhorn, Winnie Tsen, and Jason Wildhagen made important contributions to this report.

GAO's Mission	The Government Accountability Office, the audit, evaluation, and investigative arm of Congress, exists to support Congress in meeting its constitutional responsibilities and to help improve the performance and accountability of the federal government for the American people. GAO examines the use of public funds; evaluates federal programs and policies; and provides analyses, recommendations, and other assistance to help Congress make informed oversight, policy, and funding decisions. GAO's commitment to good government is reflected in its core values of accountability, integrity, and reliability.
Obtaining Copies of GAO Reports and Testimony	The fastest and easiest way to obtain copies of GAO documents at no cost is through GAO's website (http://www.gao.gov). Each weekday afternoon, GAO posts on its website newly released reports, testimony, and correspondence. To have GAO e-mail you a list of newly posted products, go to http://www.gao.gov and select "E-mail Updates."
Order by Phone	The price of each GAO publication reflects GAO's actual cost of production and distribution and depends on the number of pages in the publication and whether the publication is printed in color or black and white. Pricing and ordering information is posted on GAO's website, http://www.gao.gov/ordering.htm.
	Place orders by calling (202) 512-6000, toll free (866) 801-7077, or TDD (202) 512-2537.
	Orders may be paid for using American Express, Discover Card, MasterCard, Visa, check, or money order. Call for additional information.
Connect with GAO	Connect with GAO on Facebook, Flickr, Twitter, and YouTube. Subscribe to our RSS Feeds or E-mail Updates. Listen to our Podcasts. Visit GAO on the web at www.gao.gov.
To Report Fraud, Waste, and Abuse in Federal Programs	Contact: Website: http://www.gao.gov/fraudnet/fraudnet.htm E-mail: fraudnet@gao.gov Automated answering system: (800) 424-5454 or (202) 512-7470
Congressional Relations	Katherine Siggerud, Managing Director, siggerudk@gao.gov, (202) 512-4400, U.S. Government Accountability Office, 441 G Street NW, Room 7125, Washington, DC 20548
Public Affairs	Chuck Young, Managing Director, youngc1@gao.gov, (202) 512-4800 U.S. Government Accountability Office, 441 G Street NW, Room 7149 Washington, DC 20548

Please Print on Recycled Paper.